The Echo Show 21 Guide

Entertainment & Productivity in One Smart Display

Unlock Fire TV, Alexa Integration, and Smart Home Control for Your Kitchen or Office with the Revolutionary 21-inch Screen

Kylan P.crook

TABLE OF CONTENT

Introduction

The Echo Show 21 stands as a monumental leap forward in the world of smart home displays. With its massive 21-inch touchscreen, it brings a perfect fusion of entertainment, productivity, and smart home control into any space it inhabits. Whether it's your kitchen, office, or living room, this device offers a commanding presence, changing the way we interact with technology. But what exactly is the Echo Show 21, and why has it created so much buzz? In this introduction, we will dive into the purpose behind this new smart display, why it's capturing the attention of tech enthusiasts, and who would benefit most from having it in their home or workspace.

The Echo Show 21 is part of Amazon's expanding lineup of Echo devices, designed to make your life smarter, more convenient, and more entertaining. It's an upgraded version of the Echo Show 15, but with a significant twist: its larger 21-inch screen makes it an ideal addition for anyone looking to elevate their space with both functionality and style.

This device isn't just a digital assistant; it's a versatile smart display that integrates Alexa's powerful capabilities, a built-in Fire TV, and offers robust smart home controls. The screen size itself makes a huge difference in usability, allowing for an enhanced viewing experience, whether you're cooking in the kitchen, attending video calls, or simply enjoying your favorite shows.

So, why should you care about the Echo Show 21? In short, it brings unparalleled convenience, functionality, and entertainment right to the heart of your home. It serves not only as a high-quality display for media consumption but also as a smart home hub.

With the ability to control lights, security systems, music, and more with voice commands, the Echo Show 21 empowers you to simplify and streamline everyday tasks. If you've ever wished for a device that can do it all—from streaming Netflix to helping you organize your day—this might be exactly what you've been waiting for.

Now, who exactly should consider using the Echo Show 21? If you're someone who loves integrating smart tech into your home, enjoys watching TV or movies, or simply wants to add some productivity to your workspace, then this device is worth considering. It's particularly ideal for small spaces where traditional TVs and devices might be too cumbersome. Imagine a digital assistant with a screen that allows you to view your calendar, follow along with recipes, and check in on your smart home devices—all without leaving the kitchen.

Additionally, anyone who is passionate about smart home technology will appreciate how the Echo Show 21 doubles as a hub for controlling all connected devices.

Whether you're a tech-savvy homeowner looking to integrate a seamless smart home experience or someone who wants an entertainment setup that also improves your daily efficiency, the Echo Show 21 provides something for everyone. It's not just a piece of tech; it's a way of enhancing your lifestyle in a highly intuitive and user-friendly way.

In the following sections, we'll delve deeper into its features, the innovative integration with Fire TV and Alexa, and explore how it transforms everyday tasks into something more interactive and enjoyable. So, if you're ready to learn how the Echo Show 21 can be a game-changer for your home or office, keep reading.

Chapter 1: The Evolution of Echo Show

From Echo Show 10 to Echo Show 21

The Echo Show series began with a simple idea: integrating Alexa with a screen for more interactive smart home management. The first Echo Show was revolutionary at the time, as it allowed users to not only interact with Alexa through voice commands but also visually engage with their smart devices, watch videos, make video calls, and more. However, as time passed, Amazon realized that the market demanded more from these smart displays—more versatility, better performance, and larger screens.

The Echo Show 10 was a significant leap forward in this evolution. Featuring a 10.1-inch display that could rotate, the Echo Show 10 added a unique dimension to the concept of a smart display. It could follow your movements around the room, making it more interactive for users who were busy cooking in the kitchen or moving around their living rooms. This model was a hit, with its improved audio quality and user-friendly experience, but there was one limitation: the size of the screen.

While the 10-inch screen was suitable for a variety of tasks, users began asking for something bigger—something that could be a true centerpiece of their living space. Amazon responded to this demand with the Echo Show 15, a model with a 15.6-inch display. The Show 15 was a noticeable step up in terms of screen size, but it still didn't meet the expectations of many who wanted a more immersive, cinematic experience.

Why the Echo Show 15 Was Discontinued

Despite its potential, the Echo Show 15 didn't gain the traction Amazon hoped for. One major issue was that it still wasn't large enough for those looking to use the device primarily for entertainment. The smaller screen felt limiting in larger spaces, and users found that while the Show 15 could do many things well, it didn't truly excel at being a smart home entertainment hub.

The Echo Show 15 also had some shortcomings in the audio department. While the display was visually impressive, the sound quality wasn't on par with expectations for a device meant to replace a TV. Additionally, the lack of robust Fire TV integration made it feel more like a digital picture frame than a full-fledged entertainment device. While its size made it better suited for rooms like the kitchen or office, its smaller screen and inconsistent performance made it less than ideal for those hoping to use it as a TV replacement.

Ultimately, Amazon decided to discontinue the Echo Show 15 in favor of creating a more powerful and versatile model. Enter the Echo Show 21—designed to overcome the limitations of its predecessor and offer users a truly immersive, all-in-one smart display experience.

The Need for a Larger, More Powerful Smart Display

With the discontinuation of the Echo Show 15, Amazon set out to create something that could meet the diverse needs of its users. The Echo Show 21, with its 21-inch screen, was developed to provide a larger display suitable for more spacious rooms. This device wasn't just a minor upgrade from the Echo Show 15; it was a complete rethinking of what a smart display could be.

The decision to go with a 21-inch screen was a direct response to the growing demand for devices that could double as entertainment hubs without compromising on performance.

Many consumers wanted a screen large enough to use for streaming, video calls, and smart home controls, but they didn't want the bulky presence of a traditional TV. The Echo Show 21 strikes a perfect balance. It's big enough to deliver a satisfying visual experience but compact enough to fit comfortably in kitchens, living rooms, and offices.

Besides just the screen size, the Echo Show 21 comes with improved audio that makes it a truly immersive device. Users have noted the significant difference in sound quality compared to previous models, particularly with the bass, which now feels fuller and more powerful. This makes it ideal for streaming shows, listening to music, or even watching recipes in the kitchen while you cook.

Whether you're making a video call to a friend or watching your favorite show, the Echo Show

21 offers a richer, more enjoyable audio-visual experience.

Moreover, the Echo Show 21 doesn't just meet the demands for better size and sound—it's built with cutting-edge technology. The device comes equipped with Wi-Fi 6E, ensuring faster and more reliable internet connections. This is particularly important in a time when smart homes are becoming more connected, and devices need to work seamlessly with one another. With Wi-Fi 6E, users can enjoy buffer-free streaming, faster smart device controls, and more responsive interactions with Alexa.

The Echo Show 21 isn't just a larger version of its predecessors; it's a reimagined, feature-packed powerhouse designed for the modern home. Whether you're looking to upgrade your kitchen setup, need a smart assistant with a bigger screen, or want to use it as an entertainment hub, the Echo Show 21 delivers. It takes all the best features of its predecessors and amplifies them, ensuring that every aspect of your experience—from audio to video to connectivity—is top-tier.

This device isn't just a smart display; it's a solution for those who want it all—a seamless blend of entertainment, productivity, and smart home control in one. With this new model, Amazon is proving that they are not only keeping up with the latest trends in smart tech but also defining the future of the smart display category.

Chapter 2: Design, Display, and First Impressions

Unboxing the Echo Show 21

Opening the box of the Echo Show 21 feels like unveiling a piece of modern technology designed to fit seamlessly into your life. As you remove the packaging, the first thing you notice is the absence of excess material. Amazon has clearly put thought into minimizing waste, with the device snugly placed in a custom-cut foam insert to ensure that it arrives in perfect condition.

Inside the box, you'll find the Echo Show 21 itself, a power adapter, and a quick-start guide that walks you through the setup process. The adapter is robust and designed to provide stable power to the device, while the guide is straightforward, highlighting the simple steps to get you started. You won't need to spend much time getting everything ready, as the setup process is incredibly user-friendly. There are no complicated cables to worry about, and you'll have the device running within minutes of taking it out of the box.

For those familiar with previous Echo Show models, the process will be familiar, but even for first-time buyers, the Echo Show 21 is intuitive enough that anyone can set it up without a hitch. Once you plug in the power adapter and connect to Wi-Fi, Alexa is ready to guide you through the rest. You'll also receive an included Fire TV remote, a welcome addition that allows you to control the device like a traditional TV, adding an extra layer of convenience for those who use it for streaming.

A Closer Look at the 21-inch Display

When it comes to smart displays, size truly matters, and the Echo Show 21 delivers in a way that its predecessors couldn't. The 21-inch screen is an absolute standout, offering a much larger canvas for whatever you need to view. Whether it's streaming your favorite shows, browsing through recipes, or displaying your photos, the display is large enough to make a significant impact without being overwhelmingly bulky.

The resolution on the Echo Show 21 is crystal clear, offering vibrant colors and sharp details. With a high-definition display, it provides an immersive viewing experience. Watching a cooking show or looking at high-resolution photos from your Amazon Photos library will feel like you're watching on a much larger screen. The display's clarity enhances the overall experience, making it a joy to use whether you're using it for practical purposes, like viewing recipes while you cook, or more leisure activities like watching YouTube or Netflix.

Unlike smaller smart displays, the larger screen doesn't just feel like a passive viewing experience. The screen size allows for better multitasking. You can have multiple widgets, like weather, news, and a shopping list, visible at once, and still have enough screen real estate left for whatever you want to view. Whether you're interacting with Alexa for daily tasks or just relaxing with your favorite media, the Echo Show 21's screen provides a detailed, bright, and immersive experience.

The viewing angles are another highlight. Whether you're sitting, standing, or walking around the room, the 21-inch display remains clear and vibrant from nearly every angle. This makes it perfect for kitchens, offices, or living rooms, where you may not always be directly in front of the device.

The Sleek and Modern Design for Any Room

Aesthetics play a significant role in the design of any smart device, and the Echo Show 21 stands out in this department. The device's sleek, minimalist design makes it a perfect fit for a variety of spaces. Its clean lines and elegant profile allow it to blend in with nearly any room's decor, whether you're placing it in your kitchen, office, or living room. It's large enough to make a statement but not so large that it feels out of place.

The frame of the Echo Show 21 is thin, with a matte finish that gives it a sophisticated look. It feels premium to the touch and doesn't draw attention away from the content on the screen. The display is mounted at an optimal angle to make sure you have a clear view of whatever you're watching, and the device is surprisingly sturdy given its size.

Whether it's resting on a countertop or sitting on a shelf, the Echo Show 21 remains stable and secure.

What's more, the Echo Show 21 integrates perfectly with Amazon's broader smart home ecosystem. It can be mounted on the wall or placed on a countertop, depending on your space. Its design allows it to serve as more than just a smart display; it can act as the control hub for your smart home devices. Whether you're adjusting the thermostat, dimming the lights, or controlling security cameras, you can do it all with just a tap or voice command.

The interface is also incredibly user-friendly. The home screen features a clean layout with easy-to-navigate icons. You can access your most frequently used apps, including music and video streaming services, with just a swipe. The touch interface is responsive and smooth, making it easy to switch between different tasks without frustration.

The Echo Show 21 is designed not only to function seamlessly but also to fit into your daily life without clashing with your decor. It strikes a perfect balance between practicality and aesthetics, providing a functional and stylish addition to your home.

In the Echo Show 21, Amazon has created more than just a smart display; it's a device that fits into your home, elevates your space, and simplifies your everyday tasks. Whether you're looking for a device to enhance your productivity or to serve as a smart entertainment hub, the Echo Show 21 offers everything you need in a sleek, easy-to-use design. It's a perfect blend of functionality, design, and technology that enhances any room it occupies.

Chapter 3: Fire TV Built-In: Revolutionizing Entertainment

Streaming with Fire TV on the Echo Show 21

The addition of Fire TV integration to the Echo Show 21 completely revolutionizes the device, transforming it from a basic smart display into a full-fledged entertainment hub. With Fire TV built right into the Echo Show 21, it becomes an all-in-one device that allows you to stream movies, TV shows, sports, and much more, directly from the screen.

This means you no longer need to rely on external streaming boxes or smart TVs; the Echo Show 21 is a self-sufficient, compact entertainment system. The process of accessing your favourite content is streamlined and efficient. Whether you're in the kitchen cooking dinner or working from your home office, you can instantly jump into a movie or TV show with minimal effort. The integration of Fire TV is smooth, with the user interface designed to mimic the traditional Fire TV experience, providing familiarity for those who are already accustomed to the Fire TV platform.

By turning your Echo Show 21 into an entertainment hub, Amazon has added significant value to the device. With a screen that's perfect for personal viewing, the device delivers a rich media experience. The large, vibrant display ensures that your streaming content looks sharp and clear, while the sound quality (improved compared to previous Echo Show models) fills the room with rich audio. The 21-inch screen gives you a spacious viewing area, allowing you to enjoy your favorite shows without squinting at a small screen.

Voice Commands for Seamless Entertainment

The Echo Show 21 doesn't just excel at displaying content — it's also designed to make managing your entertainment as effortless as possible, thanks to Alexa's voice control. Instead of fumbling with remote controls or navigating through clunky menus, you can simply speak to Alexa to control nearly every aspect of your media experience.

Need a specific show? Just say, "Alexa, play *The Office* on Netflix," and the Echo Show 21 will search, find, and start the show instantly. Want to pause the movie while you grab a snack? A simple "Alexa, pause" will halt playback without you needing to pick up a remote. And if you're unsure what to watch, Alexa can even make suggestions based on your preferences. For instance, if you frequently watch sci-fi movies, Alexa might suggest the latest releases in that genre, making it easier for you to discover new content.

Voice commands go beyond just media control. You can also adjust the volume, fast forward or rewind, and switch between apps with simple, intuitive commands. The integration of Alexa's voice assistant ensures that you're not tied to the device itself — your voice is your remote, providing a hands-free experience that's incredibly convenient when you're busy with other tasks. Whether you're cooking, cleaning, or just relaxing, controlling your entertainment has never been more effortless.

Popular Apps and Streaming Services Available

One of the major benefits of the Fire TV integration is the wide range of streaming services and apps that are now available directly on the Echo Show 21. Whether you're a fan of Netflix, Amazon Prime Video, Hulu, or other popular streaming platforms, this smart display has access to all the content you love.

For Netflix users, you can easily access your library of TV shows, movies, and original series. Prime Video users will enjoy access to Amazon's massive library of content, including exclusive Amazon Originals. Hulu is available for those who prefer their streaming service for television shows and movies, offering a large variety of on-demand content. Additionally, the Echo Show 21 supports Disney+, making it a go-to option for family entertainment, with access to both classic and new Disney films and series.

Beyond the major streaming giants, the Fire TV integration on the Echo Show 21 also provides access to other popular apps, including YouTube, Apple TV+, Sling TV, and more. With these services, you can keep up with the latest trends, watch live events, and catch up on the shows you missed. The best part? All these services are conveniently housed in a single interface that's easy to navigate, making it quick and easy to jump between apps and find what you're looking for.

For those who enjoy live TV or want to keep up with the latest news and sports, the Echo Show 21 has apps like ESPN and news networks, such as CNN and BBC. You can stay connected with live updates while cooking dinner or organizing your workspace, all thanks to the vast app ecosystem available.

The seamless integration of these popular streaming services makes the Echo Show 21 an essential device for anyone who enjoys entertainment but doesn't want the hassle of managing multiple devices or cables. It's the ultimate multitasking device, offering convenience and a great viewing experience all in one.

By incorporating Fire TV, Amazon has turned the Echo Show 21 into a powerhouse for entertainment, giving you access to an endless array of content with just your voice.

The integration of streaming services, voice commands, and the large, vibrant display make it a perfect addition to any home. Whether you're looking for a device to watch movies, catch up on shows, or simply enjoy some music, the Echo Show 21 offers it all, all while providing the added benefit of seamless integration with Alexa for effortless control.

Chapter 4: Alexa Integration: A Smart Assistant at Your Service

Voice-Controlled Convenience with Alexa

Alexa is more than just a voice assistant — it's your virtual helper that brings convenience and efficiency to your daily life. The integration of Alexa in the Echo Show 21 allows you to control a variety of tasks with just your voice, making everything from managing your entertainment to controlling your smart home devices incredibly easy.

With voice commands, Alexa helps you navigate your day effortlessly. Need to check the weather before you head out? Just ask, "Alexa, what's the weather like today?" and she'll provide an instant update. Want to play music while you cook? "Alexa, play jazz music" is all it takes.

The voice recognition is fast and accurate, so you don't have to repeat commands or struggle to get a response.

But Alexa's capabilities extend far beyond simple queries. With the Echo Show 21, Alexa can control your entire environment, making it a versatile tool for your home or office. Whether you're asking Alexa to play your favorite podcast while you work or requesting a quick answer to a question, the device adapts to your needs and works efficiently with you throughout the day. The Echo Show 21's integration with Alexa transforms it from a smart display to a dynamic assistant, streamlining how you interact with technology.

Managing Smart Home Devices with Alexa

One of Alexa's standout features is its ability to manage your smart home devices. If your home is equipped with smart lights, thermostats, or even security systems, Alexa integrates seamlessly with these devices, offering you hands-free control. This is where the Echo Show 21 shines as more than just a display — it becomes a hub for managing your smart home.

Imagine this scenario: you're cooking dinner, and you realize the lights in the living room are still on. Instead of leaving the kitchen to turn them off, you can simply ask Alexa, "Alexa, turn off the living room lights," and she will comply instantly. Or perhaps it's a chilly evening, and you want to adjust the thermostat to warm up the house. A quick command like, "Alexa, set the thermostat to 72 degrees," and your home is immediately more comfortable. Alexa makes it simple to manage your environment without ever having to lift a finger.

The Echo Show 21 also allows you to group devices for easier control.

If you have several smart bulbs or plugs, you can create a "room" in the Alexa app and control them all at once. This integration eliminates the need for multiple remotes or apps, bringing everything into one streamlined interface. The combination of Alexa and smart home features elevates the Echo Show 21 as a central piece of your connected ecosystem, allowing you to control almost every aspect of your home with a single voice command.

Alexa's Ability to Manage Tasks and Reminders

In addition to controlling your home environment, Alexa is a master of organization. With the Echo Show 21, Alexa can manage your tasks and help you stay on top of your schedule throughout the day. Whether you need to set reminders, alarms, or even check your calendar, Alexa can handle it all with ease.

For example, you could say, "Alexa, set a reminder to call mom at 3 p.m." and she will notify you at the designated time. Or, if you're juggling multiple tasks and need help staying on track, Alexa can remind you of important events and deadlines. She can even alert you when it's time to take a break, so you can stay productive without overworking yourself.

Alexa's reminder system is particularly useful for busy households or individuals with packed schedules. The Echo Show 21 makes managing your day hands-free by offering constant access to reminders, to-do lists, and alarms. Additionally, you can ask Alexa to provide a summary of your schedule, making it easy to stay organized without having to consult a planner or your phone.

The versatility of Alexa's task management capabilities is evident in how it allows you to be more productive while freeing up your time to focus on other things.

Whether you're coordinating family activities or keeping track of work commitments, Alexa is an invaluable tool for staying organized.

Making Video Calls with Alexa

The Echo Show 21 isn't just a hub for voice commands and smart home control — it also excels in communication. Thanks to its enhanced camera, making video calls has never been easier or clearer. The integration of Alexa with the camera system enables you to connect with loved ones, friends, or colleagues with just a few voice commands.

The camera on the Echo Show 21 offers impressive clarity, making your video calls crisp and detailed. Whether you're catching up with family or discussing business matters, the experience is smooth and professional. You can simply say, "Alexa, call John on Zoom," and the call will initiate automatically.

Thanks to Alexa's voice recognition and the Echo Show's seamless interface, managing calls is hassle-free.

One of the best features of video calling with Alexa is the ability to make calls between other Echo devices. If you have family or friends who also own Echo devices, you can easily connect with them, even if they are miles away. This makes the Echo Show 21 a perfect tool for staying in touch with loved ones, especially for those who don't have access to other video-calling platforms.

The larger 21-inch display enhances the video call experience, providing a wide viewing area that ensures everyone in the room can participate in the conversation. Whether you're using it for casual chats or business meetings, the Echo Show 21 provides a professional-level video calling solution, all controlled by voice commands.

The Echo Show 21, with its integration of Alexa, offers more than just a smart display — it's a complete personal assistant that simplifies and enriches your life.

From managing your smart home to staying organized and connected through video calls, the Echo Show 21 makes life easier and more efficient. Alexa's capabilities truly shine in how seamlessly it integrates with your daily tasks, helping you maintain productivity and stay connected without ever needing to touch a button. Whether you're looking to control your home environment, stay on top of your schedule, or simply connect with others, Alexa is the intelligent companion you can rely on.

Chapter 5: Audio and Camera Enhancement

Improved Audio Quality for a Richer Experience

The Echo Show 21 takes a significant leap forward in audio performance. Whether you're watching your favorite TV show, listening to music, or attending a virtual meeting, the sound experience is noticeably better than its predecessors. One of the standout features of this device is the enhanced audio system, which delivers richer bass, clearer treble, and an overall more immersive sound.

In comparison to the Echo Show 15, the 21-inch model boasts upgraded speakers that produce a fuller, more dynamic sound. Whether you're cooking in the kitchen or relaxing in the living room, the improved audio fills the space more effectively. This upgrade isn't just about volume; it's about clarity and depth. Even at lower volumes, the sound remains crisp, making it ideal for casual listening or background music. The bass, in particular, stands out, making music sound fuller and more balanced, while voices in shows and movies are sharper, without being drowned out by background noise.

This improvement in audio quality is especially noticeable when using the Echo Show 21 for entertainment purposes. Streaming services like Netflix, Hulu, or Amazon Prime Video sound much richer, providing an experience that's closer to what you'd expect from high-quality speakers. The device's spatial audio capabilities make watching content feel more immersive, creating an atmosphere that pulls you into the action.

Whether you're cooking and want to hear your favorite playlist clearly or catching up on a TV show with family, the improved sound enhances the overall experience.

The Upgraded Camera for Better Video Calls

The Echo Show 21's camera has also received a significant upgrade, making video calls clearer and more natural. Unlike its predecessor, the Echo Show 15, which had a basic camera, the 21-inch model features a much more advanced system designed to improve your video communication. One of the most notable enhancements is the wider field of view, which ensures that more people can fit comfortably within the frame.

Whether you're talking to a friend, holding a business meeting, or connecting with family, the wider view ensures that everyone is included in the conversation.

The upgraded camera offers clearer, more detailed images, which make a significant difference during video calls.

The enhanced resolution and larger viewing area help eliminate awkward cropping, ensuring that your face, and the faces of others, are visible without the need for constant adjustments.

This is especially important when you're using the Echo Show 21 in spaces like the kitchen or living room, where you might want to talk while multitasking. The camera automatically adjusts for optimal clarity, even if you're not sitting perfectly still or directly in front of the device.

Another feature that improves your video calling experience is the camera's enhanced zoom capabilities. This allows you to focus on the people you're talking to or bring the camera closer to show something important, such as a recipe or a document.

Whether you're explaining a process or just catching up with friends, the camera ensures that your calls are more interactive and engaging, offering a more immersive experience than ever before.

Privacy Features: Camera Cover and More

While the Echo Show 21 excels in audio and video, it also offers important privacy features to ensure that your personal data remains secure. The camera, which is crucial for video calls and security purposes, comes with a built-in privacy cover that can be easily activated with a simple voice command. When you want to ensure that no one is watching or recording, you can say, "Alexa, turn off the camera," or manually slide the cover over the lens.

This feature provides peace of mind, knowing that your privacy is always under your control.

In addition to the camera cover, the Echo Show 21 includes several other privacy measures that make it an ideal choice for those who are particularly concerned about data security.

You can review and manage your voice recordings directly through the Alexa app, allowing you to delete any stored interactions if you prefer. This feature helps maintain control over your voice data and prevents unwanted or unnecessary recordings.

Furthermore, the Echo Show 21's microphone can also be turned off when you want to ensure that Alexa isn't listening in on your conversations. With a simple toggle on the device or through the app, you can disable the mic entirely, preventing Alexa from responding to any commands. This is especially useful when you're not using the device, offering an extra layer of security and peace of mind.

The privacy features go beyond just the camera and microphone. The Echo Show 21 allows you to set up additional security settings to limit the data Alexa collects. You can customize the device to work in a way that aligns with your privacy preferences, ensuring that you're always in control of what's shared and stored.

The Echo Show 21 not only delivers impressive upgrades in audio and video performance but also ensures that your privacy remains protected. With superior sound quality, a wide-view camera, and built-in privacy features, this smart display offers an enhanced user experience that is both functional and secure.

Whether you're enjoying your favorite music, catching up with loved ones through clear video calls, or simply using the device to control your smart home, the Echo Show 21 excels at creating a seamless, enriched environment. And with its robust privacy features, you can trust that your data and personal space are always secure, giving you the ultimate peace of mind while you enjoy all the benefits this innovative device has to offer.

Chapter 6: Setting Up Echo Show 21

Step-by-Step Setup: Getting Started

Setting up the Echo Show 21 is a quick and straightforward process, and the experience has been streamlined to ensure even those who aren't particularly tech-savvy can enjoy their new device in no time. Right out of the box, the Echo Show 21 is designed for ease of use. After plugging in the device, you'll be prompted to follow a series of on-screen instructions that guide you through the initial setup. The device automatically powers on once it's plugged in, and you'll be greeted by a friendly setup screen that walks you through the essential steps.

First, you'll be asked to select your preferred language and region, which helps tailor the device's voice recognition and services to your location. After that, the Echo Show 21 will connect to your Wi-Fi network. The device supports Wi-Fi 6, so you should expect faster speeds and more reliable connections, even in households with multiple devices connected. You can easily input your Wi-Fi credentials via the touchscreen, and the device will connect almost instantly.

Next, you'll be prompted to log in to your Amazon account. This step is necessary for activating the device and syncing it with your Amazon services, including Amazon Photos, Prime Video, and Alexa. Once logged in, the device will automatically configure the rest of your settings, like time zone and weather preferences, based on your location.

After completing the basic setup, the Echo Show 21 will ask if you want to connect it to Alexa. The device is designed to work seamlessly with Alexa, and the setup process for Alexa is straightforward.

If you've already set up an Alexa device in your home, the Echo Show 21 should sync with your existing Alexa setup, allowing you to control other devices, play music, or ask questions right away.

With the initial setup completed, you'll be ready to start exploring all the features that make the Echo Show 21 such a versatile device.

Pairing Alexa, Fire TV, and Smart Devices

Once you've completed the basic setup, the next step is to pair your Echo Show 21 with other smart devices around your home or office. The Echo Show 21 acts as a powerful hub for your smart home, allowing you to control various devices, such as smart lights, thermostats, and locks, all from a central screen.

To get started, simply open the Alexa app on your phone or use the device's touchscreen to access the smart home section.

From here, you can add compatible devices by selecting the "Devices" tab and choosing "Add Device." Alexa will automatically search for nearby devices, including any that are already Alexa-enabled, like smart bulbs or plugs. The setup process is intuitive, with the app providing clear instructions on how to connect each device. For example, if you have a Philips Hue light bulb, the app will guide you through the process of pairing the bulb with your Echo Show 21 via your Wi-Fi network.

For devices that don't support automatic pairing, you can manually enter setup codes or connect them through third-party apps. Once connected, you can control these devices directly from the Echo Show 21's touchscreen or by giving Alexa voice commands.

For example, you can say, "Alexa, turn on the lights" or "Alexa, set the thermostat to 72 degrees," and Alexa will take care of the rest.

Pairing the Fire TV with your Echo Show 21 takes only a few more steps. Since the Fire TV is built directly into the device, you don't need to worry about an extra setup process. However, if you have a separate Fire TV Stick or Fire TV Cube, you can link those devices to your Echo Show 21 by going to the "Devices" tab in the Alexa app. Simply select the Fire TV device, and Alexa will pair it automatically.

Once paired, you can use the Echo Show 21's screen to control and stream content from your Fire TV, giving you access to a wealth of streaming options right at your fingertips.

The ease with which the Echo Show 21 integrates with Alexa-enabled devices and Fire TV is one of the reasons why it's considered a game-changer in smart home technology.

Navigating the Interface and Customizing Settings

Now that your Echo Show 21 is set up and paired with your devices, it's time to explore the interface and customize settings to your liking. The device boasts a large 21-inch touchscreen that offers an intuitive, user-friendly experience, making navigation simple and enjoyable.

Upon waking the device from sleep, you'll be greeted by a home screen that offers a variety of customizable widgets. These widgets provide at-a-glance information, such as the weather, time, and news, and they can be rearranged to fit your needs. You can easily swipe left or right to scroll through different screens, and touching the screen allows you to interact with various apps, like Fire TV, music, photos, or smart home controls.

The settings menu can be accessed by swiping down from the top of the screen, where you'll find options to adjust device volume, screen brightness, and more.

In the settings menu, you can also change your Wi-Fi settings, add new Alexa skills, or manage your linked devices. If you prefer a darker look, there's an option to switch the display to "dark mode," which makes the interface easier on the eyes during nighttime use.

One of the key features that make the Echo Show 21 so versatile is the ability to customize the display settings. You can choose a background image for the home screen or link the device to your Amazon Photos account to display a rotating selection of your own photos. This gives the device a personalized touch, making it feel like a part of your home rather than just another tech gadget.

Additionally, you can manage Alexa's voice settings, adjust privacy features, and even set up routines to automate actions.

For example, you can create a routine that automatically turns on the lights and starts playing your favorite morning playlist as soon as you say, "Alexa, good morning." Customizing the settings allows you to get the most out of your Echo Show 21, tailoring the experience to your specific needs.

The setup process for the Echo Show 21 is designed to be quick, simple, and intuitive, allowing you to get started without any hassle. Pairing with Alexa-enabled devices and Fire TV is a breeze, and the interface is easy to navigate, with plenty of customization options to make the device feel like your own.

Whether you're managing smart home devices, streaming content, or adjusting settings, the

Echo Show 21 offers a seamless and enjoyable experience that's tailored to fit your lifestyle.

Chapter 7: The Pros and Cons of Echo Show 21

Why the Echo Show 21 Stands Out

The Echo Show 21 immediately distinguishes itself from its predecessors and competitors with its impressive 21-inch display. This large screen size is perfect for a wide range of use cases, from streaming content in a kitchen to video calling in an office or living room. Unlike its smaller siblings, which might be more suited for tight spaces, the Echo Show 21 feels like a true centerpiece that can enhance any room's aesthetics while providing exceptional utility.

One of the standout features of the Echo Show 21 is the seamless integration of Fire TV. This built-in feature turns the device into a mini entertainment hub, allowing users to stream movies, TV shows, and even live sports directly from the display.

By combining the power of Fire TV with Alexa's voice control, the Echo Show 21 offers a hands-free, immersive experience that many smaller smart displays lack. Instead of using a remote or navigating a complicated menu, users can simply speak to Alexa to access their favorite streaming apps, search for content, and control playback.

Another defining feature is Alexa's integration. Beyond simple voice commands, Alexa on the Echo Show 21 can perform a wide range of tasks, including managing smart home devices, answering questions, setting reminders, and more. The 21-inch touchscreen works in tandem with voice commands to provide an intuitive experience that makes it easy for users to interact with and control various functions.

This level of convenience and functionality is what truly sets the Echo Show 21 apart in the competitive world of smart displays.

Additionally, the Echo Show 21's design is sleek and modern, making it a natural fit for a variety of spaces. Whether placed on a kitchen counter, in a living room, or an office, its minimalist design ensures that it blends seamlessly into its environment while providing the necessary functionality.

Possible Limitations and Areas for Improvement

While the Echo Show 21 is undeniably impressive, there are some limitations that potential buyers should be aware of before making a purchase. One of the most notable concerns is its price. At a premium cost, the Echo Show 21 sits at the higher end of the smart display market.

This could be a potential deterrent for those who are on a budget or who are considering other smart displays with smaller screen sizes that may come at a lower price point. For example, the Echo Show 10 and Echo Show 8, while smaller in size, still offer many of the same features at a more affordable cost.

The size of the Echo Show 21 also presents a potential drawback for some users. While the large display is fantastic for certain rooms, it may be impractical in smaller spaces or for those who need a more compact option. The sheer size of the 21-inch screen could be overwhelming in smaller kitchens, bedrooms, or offices where users might prefer a device that takes up less space but still provides a solid smart display experience.

Another limitation worth mentioning is the lack of portability. Unlike smaller devices like the Echo Show 8, which can be easily moved from room to room or taken on the go, the Echo Show 21 is designed to remain stationary.

This means that users who want a more portable device for travel or on-the-go use may not find the Echo Show 21 to be the ideal choice.

In terms of performance, while the Echo Show 21 excels in most areas, there are occasional reports of slower responsiveness or connection issues with Wi-Fi. However, these are generally rare and may be related to specific network configurations or environmental factors, rather than being a systemic issue with the device itself. The presence of Wi-Fi 6 does help mitigate these issues, but it's still something to keep in mind for users in areas with spotty internet connections.

Finally, some users may find the built-in Fire TV remote to be a bit unnecessary, especially since Alexa's voice control can handle most media-related tasks. For those who prefer using their voice for every action, the remote might be redundant, and its inclusion could be seen as an extra expense that isn't fully leveraged.

Comparing Echo Show 21 to Other Smart Displays

When comparing the Echo Show 21 to other smart displays on the market, several key factors come into play that determine why it might be the best choice for certain users.

The most obvious distinction is the size. The Echo Show 21's 21-inch display far exceeds the typical 8- to 15-inch screens of most other smart displays, such as the Echo Show 10 or Echo Show 8. While these smaller devices may be more suitable for certain use cases, the larger screen offers a more immersive experience for watching shows, video chatting, and controlling smart home devices.

Users who prioritize screen size and resolution may find the Echo Show 21 the best choice for larger rooms or as a home entertainment centerpiece.

Another aspect worth considering is the integration of Fire TV. While other smart displays like the Echo Show 10 or the Google Nest Hub may support streaming services, the Echo Show 21's direct Fire TV integration offers a more robust entertainment experience. Unlike other displays that require additional hardware or apps to stream media, the Echo Show 21 has Fire TV built right into the device, making it a more seamless option for streaming content. This integration ensures that users have access to popular apps like Netflix, Amazon Prime Video, Hulu, and more, all accessible through voice commands or touchscreen interaction.

In comparison to Google's Nest Hub Max, which has a similarly-sized screen, the Echo Show 21 stands out with Alexa's advanced capabilities.

Alexa, compared to Google Assistant, offers a more extensive range of features, from smart home management to third-party app integration, making it a more versatile assistant. Additionally, Alexa's voice control is more reliable when it comes to handling complex tasks such as controlling Fire TV or managing smart home devices.

While other brands may offer similar functionalities, the Echo Show 21's combination of a large screen, voice integration, and Fire TV support makes it a compelling choice for users who want both entertainment and productivity from a single device.

The Echo Show 21 is a standout product in the world of smart displays, but it's not without its limitations. The larger screen, Fire TV integration, and advanced Alexa features make it an exceptional device for those looking for an all-in-one smart display that excels in both entertainment and productivity.

However, its price point and size may not be suitable for everyone, and it's important to consider how these factors align with your specific needs. Comparing the Echo Show 21 to other devices in the market shows that it holds a strong advantage in its niche, offering users a unique blend of size, functionality, and seamless integration with Alexa and Fire TV.

Chapter 8: Conclusion and Final Thoughts

Who Should Buy the Echo Show 21?

The Echo Show 21 is not just another smart display. It is a high-performance device designed to enhance both entertainment and productivity, making it ideal for users who want more than just a simple screen. This device is best suited for individuals or families looking for a large screen display that doubles as a mini entertainment center, with the added benefit of smart home control and voice-activated convenience.

If you are someone who spends a lot of time in the kitchen or living room, the Echo Show 21 can be an excellent addition to your space. Its large 21-inch display makes it perfect for watching cooking tutorials, streaming your favorite shows while preparing meals, or even displaying your favorite photos as a dynamic photo frame when not in use. The seamless integration of Fire TV allows you to access a range of entertainment services right from the device, meaning you don't need to juggle multiple gadgets to enjoy movies and TV shows.

On the other hand, if you're someone who needs a smart display primarily for quick voice queries, a smaller and more compact version of the Echo Show, like the Echo Show 8 or Echo Show 10, may suffice. The Echo Show 21's size might be a bit overwhelming for smaller spaces like a small bedroom or a desk. In those cases, the added size may not justify the cost, as the smaller models provide most of the same Alexa features and screen capabilities.

The Echo Show 21 is also an excellent choice for tech enthusiasts who want the latest features.

With built-in Fire TV integration, Wi-Fi 6E, and an upgraded camera, this device is designed to deliver a top-tier experience for those who demand premium features and performance.

Is the Upgrade Worth It from Echo Show 15?

For those already owning the Echo Show 15, the question arises: Is upgrading to the Echo Show 21 worthwhile? The Echo Show 15, with its 15-inch display, is certainly no slouch, offering many of the same smart display features that users love. However, the Echo Show 21 offers several key improvements that make it an attractive upgrade, especially for users who want a larger, more powerful device.

First, the screen size is a notable step up. The Echo Show 21 offers a 21-inch display, making it far easier to see from a distance, which is ideal for spaces like kitchens and living rooms where you might need to view the screen from across the room.

The larger screen makes streaming content, viewing recipes, or watching video calls far more comfortable. If you frequently use your Echo Show for entertainment or as a central hub for smart home control, the increased screen real estate will make a noticeable difference.

Another compelling reason to upgrade is the enhanced audio quality. The Echo Show 21 provides deeper bass and clearer sound, a significant improvement over the Echo Show 15's audio performance. If you value high-quality sound for watching videos or listening to music, the new speaker system in the Echo Show 21 is a key factor to consider.

It offers a much richer sound experience, making it better suited for full-room audio.

Additionally, the upgraded camera with a wider field of view and improved video calling functionality makes the Echo Show 21 a better choice for those who use their smart display for video calls with family, friends, or colleagues. The more advanced camera ensures clearer, more fluid video chats, which is a huge benefit for anyone who uses their Echo Show as a communication tool.

However, if you're perfectly happy with your Echo Show 15, the upgrade might not feel as essential. The Echo Show 15 still delivers good performance, and unless you're looking for the larger screen, improved audio, or enhanced camera, sticking with the Echo Show 15 may make sense for the price-conscious user. For those on the fence, the price difference between the two models might be a key consideration.

How to Get the Most Out of Your Echo Show 21

Once you've set up your Echo Show 21, it's time to explore all the amazing features it has to offer. This device is packed with hidden tricks, tips, and customization options that can elevate your experience. Let's take a look at some ways to get the most out of your new smart display.

Voice Commands for Quick Access: One of the best features of the Echo Show 21 is the seamless integration with Alexa. To make your experience even more effortless, learn the most common voice commands for controlling your smart display. You can ask Alexa to turn on your favorite shows, control smart home devices, and even set alarms or reminders—all without lifting a finger. The Echo Show 21 is designed to be completely hands-free, allowing you to focus on other tasks without interrupting your workflow.

Customizing the Display Settings: With such a large screen, customization is key. Personalize your Echo Show 21 by adjusting display settings to fit your needs.

You can tweak the brightness, choose between a variety of clock faces, or use the screen as a photo frame to showcase family photos or artwork. Additionally, you can choose different wallpaper options or integrate Amazon Photos for a personalized touch that makes your Echo Show feel more like home.

Connecting Smart Home Devices: The Echo Show 21 is an excellent hub for managing your smart home devices. Take full advantage of its capabilities by pairing it with lights, thermostats, smart plugs, and security cameras. Set up routines that allow you to control multiple devices with a single voice command. For example, you can say, "Alexa, good morning," and the Echo Show 21 will turn on the lights, adjust the thermostat, and provide you with a weather update.

This level of automation helps streamline your daily tasks, making life more convenient.

Entertainment at Your Fingertips: With Fire TV built right into the Echo Show 21, you can enjoy endless hours of entertainment with ease. Make sure you explore the full range of streaming services available on the device, including Amazon Prime Video, Netflix, Hulu, and more.

Use Alexa to search for specific titles, ask for recommendations, or even pause and resume content hands-free. If you want to watch your favorite sports, simply ask Alexa to bring up the game and enjoy live sports on your large screen.

Making Video Calls: The Echo Show 21 is perfect for staying connected with loved ones. With its improved camera and larger screen, you can make clear, crisp video calls to family, friends, or colleagues. Use Alexa to make video calls to anyone who has an Echo device or the Alexa app.

The wide-angle camera allows for a more comfortable video call experience, ensuring that everyone can be seen clearly.

Security Features: With the added camera cover and privacy controls, the Echo Show 21 ensures that your privacy is protected. Learn how to easily disable the camera when not in use or adjust the device's settings to restrict access to certain features. Taking advantage of these privacy features gives you peace of mind when it comes to using the Echo Show 21 in your home or office.

As we conclude, it's clear that the Echo Show 21 offers exceptional value to the right audience. It's perfect for users who need a powerful smart display that can serve as both an entertainment hub and a productivity assistant. Whether you're upgrading from an older Echo Show or buying one for the first time, you'll appreciate its larger screen, improved sound, and Fire TV integration.

By exploring all the features and customizing the device to fit your needs, the Echo Show 21 can become an indispensable part of your daily life, making both work and leisure more enjoyable.

Appendix

A. Glossary of Key Terms

1. **Alexa**

   Alexa is Amazon's cloud-based voice service, which powers Echo devices. It allows users to interact with their Echo device through voice commands, enabling functionalities like controlling smart home devices, setting reminders, playing music, and much more.

2. **Fire TV**

   Fire TV is Amazon's media streaming platform. Built into the Echo Show 21, it allows users to stream movies, TV shows, and other video content from popular platforms like Amazon Prime Video, Netflix, Hulu, and more.

3. **Wi-Fi 6E**

   Wi-Fi 6E is the latest generation of

Wi-Fi technology, offering faster speeds, lower latency, and improved performance in crowded environments. The Echo Show 21 supports this technology for smoother streaming and quicker response times.

4. **Smart Home Integration**

   The ability of a device like the Echo Show 21 to interact with and control other connected smart devices such as lights, thermostats, and security cameras. This integration makes managing your home easier and more efficient.

5. **Smart Display**

   A smart display is a device that integrates a screen with voice assistant capabilities, such as Alexa. These devices allow users to access visual content (e.g., videos, recipes, photos) while also utilizing voice commands for hands-free control.

6. **Wide-Angle Camera**

   A camera with a larger field of view, allowing for clearer and more inclusive video calls. The Echo Show 21 features an upgraded camera that ensures better video quality and a broader viewing angle during calls.

B. Frequently Asked Questions (FAQ)

1. **What is the size of the Echo Show 21 screen?** The Echo Show 21 boasts a 21-inch screen, making it significantly larger than previous Echo Show models, providing an immersive viewing experience.

2. **Can I use my Echo Show 21 without a Fire TV subscription?** Yes, you can still use the Echo Show 21 without a Fire TV subscription. However, the built-in Fire TV integration provides access to streaming services such as Amazon Prime Video, Netflix, and more. For premium content,

a subscription to those services would be required.

3. **How do I make video calls with the Echo Show 21?** To make video calls, simply say, "Alexa, call [contact name]," and the Echo Show 21 will initiate the call using the device's upgraded camera and microphone.

4. **Does the Echo Show 21 have privacy features?** Yes, the Echo Show 21 includes privacy features such as a built-in camera cover, allowing you to easily disable the camera when not in use. It also offers voice command privacy settings to manage what Alexa can access.

5. **Is the Echo Show 21 compatible with other smart home devices?** Yes, the Echo Show 21 is compatible with a wide variety of Alexa-enabled smart home devices, such as lights, thermostats, locks, and security

cameras. You can control all of these devices with simple voice commands.

6. **Can I change the appearance of the Echo Show 21 screen?** Yes, you can customize the screen with different clock faces, wallpapers, and display settings. You can also set it to display photos from your Amazon Photos account or use it as a digital photo frame.

C. Troubleshooting Tips

1. **Echo Show 21 Won't Connect to Wi-Fi**
   - Ensure your Wi-Fi network is active and has a stable connection.
   - Restart your router and Echo Show device.
   - Try reconnecting your Echo Show 21 to the network by going to the settings and selecting Wi-Fi options.
   - If problems persist, ensure the Echo Show is in range of your

Wi-Fi router, and that it supports Wi-Fi 6E.

2. **Alexa Isn't Responding**

   o Check if your Echo Show's microphone is muted. The microphone button should have a red light when muted.

   o Ensure Alexa is properly configured in the device settings.

   o Verify if your internet connection is active, as Alexa requires an internet connection to function.

3. **Video Call Quality Isn't Clear**

   o Ensure that the camera lens is clean.

   o If you experience poor video quality, check your Wi-Fi signal to ensure a strong, uninterrupted connection.

   o Adjust the Echo Show's camera angle for a clearer view.

4. **Fire TV Streaming Doesn't Work**

- Ensure your Fire TV subscription is active, and that you're logged into the correct account for streaming services.
- If streaming apps aren't loading properly, restart the Echo Show 21 and ensure it is connected to a strong Wi-Fi network.

D. Echo Show 21 Specifications

- **Screen Size**: 21 inches
- **Display Type**: LCD, Full HD (1080p resolution)
- **Audio**: Dual stereo speakers, enhanced bass
- **Camera**: 13 MP camera with wide-angle lens
- **Microphone**: 4-microphone array
- **Wi-Fi**: Wi-Fi 6E support
- **Operating System**: Fire OS
- **Connectivity**: Bluetooth, USB-C, HDMI input/output (optional)

- **Voice Assistant**: Alexa
- **Smart Home Integration**: Compatible with Alexa-enabled smart devices
- **Dimensions**: 18.2" x 8.9" x 6.5"
- **Weight**: 10.5 lbs

E. How to Contact Support

If you encounter any issues or need assistance with your Echo Show 21, Amazon provides robust customer support. Here's how you can reach them:

- **Customer Service Phone**: Call Amazon's customer service at 1-888-280-4331 for direct support.
- **Online Help**: Visit Amazon's help center online at www.amazon.com/help for FAQs, troubleshooting guides, and live chat support.
- **Alexa App**: Use the Alexa app on your smartphone to manage your Echo Show

21's settings and access troubleshooting options.

F. Additional Resources

For further tips and tutorials on how to maximize your Echo Show 21 experience, check out these resources:

- **Amazon's Official Echo Show 21 Page**: Explore product specifications, updates, and feature releases.
- **Alexa Skills Store**: Discover new Alexa skills that can enhance your Echo Show 21 experience, from smart home integrations to entertainment and productivity enhancements.
- **Amazon's Digital Content Library**: A hub for all things related to Fire TV, including movies, shows, and channels you can stream on your Echo Show 21.

This appendix provides essential information to ensure a smooth experience with your Echo

Show 21, whether you're troubleshooting, setting it up, or learning how to use its features to their fullest.